About Some Owls

Alixe Dique

To order additional copies of this book, contact:
Xlibris
1-800-455-039
www.xlibris.com.au
Orders@Xlibris.com.au

About Some Owls

A Reference Book written and illustrated

By *Alixe Dique*

The five illustrations
in this book are
reproduced from
the original artwork by
the author

For the children

There are many kinds of owls,
all over the earth.
And new species are still being found
in faraway uninhabited lands.

Barn owl

has reddish- brown body

and heart- shaped face.

Males' chest is white,

females' darker and heavily
spotted.

They are eighteen inches in
height.

Found in Australia,Africa,
Asia, Europe

and America; they are
"endangered".

urrowing owl

has bright yellow eyes.

His legs are feathered,

no ear tufts and a flattened

face,

white eyebrows and chin

patch,

and a brown and white

body.

Pygmy owls

live in Mexico and the U.S.A.

They are about six inches long,

and have large talons.

Pygmy swoops low to the ground,

and often hunts by day.

They are spotted brown and white.

 SCREECH OWLS,

sleep in old trees and hollows,

tho, they like to hunt from perches in open landscape.

They like to eat

insects, reptiles, small mammals, bats, mice and small birds.

They have incredible hearing, raptorial claws and curved bill.

The male makes the nest.

Screech owls like being on their own........

and many unknown types are still being discovered.......

There are twenty one living species of this particular owl,

which is usually found in the Andes.

Alisee Dique

Tawny frogmouth

can often be mistaken

for part of a tree.

They are only found in
Australia,
Tasmania and N.G.

and are mistaken for
owls.
Frogmouths are not
raptorial like owls,
but are related to the
kingfisher
and kookaburra family.

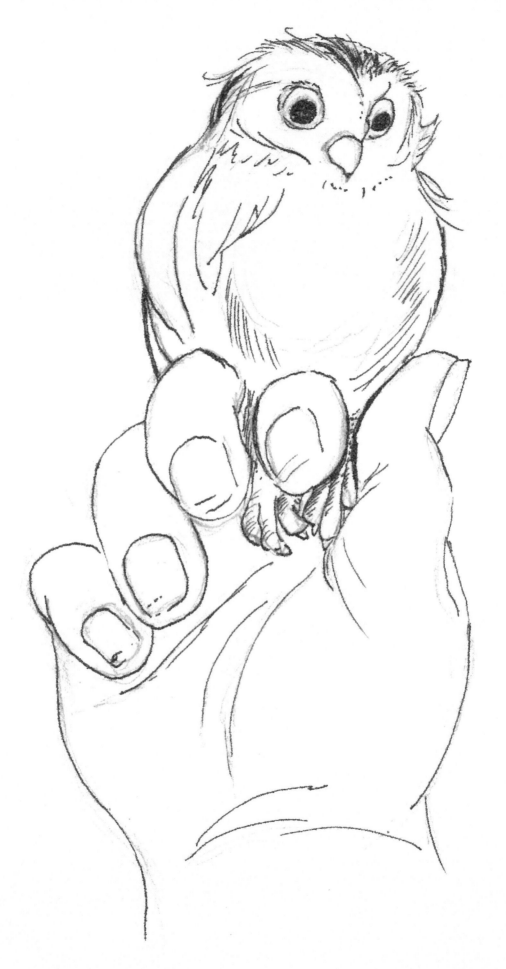

Printed in the United States
By Bookmasters